Praise for *Real Thirst*

"I found *Real Thirst* to be a slow, cool and refreshing drink. The deep singularity present within each poem, evokes a kind of *felt* suchness, and that is a *real gift.* I believe you will find these poems an antidote to the rush of your days."

~ JOHN FOX
author of *Poetic Medicine: The Healing Art of Poem-Making*
and *Finding What you Didn't Lose*

"Ivan M. Granger's poems not only invite us into reunion with the 'Thief of Hearts,' each is actually a direct infusion of that dangerous, ecstatic meeting. Every page of this book is a luminous portal through the details of this world into the vastness of pure being. I will turn to these poems again and again for transport to the ineffable, for medicine to heal my restless mind, for a fierce and tender dose of the Beloved."

~ KIM ROSEN
author of *Saved by a Poem:*
The Transformative Power of Words

"A delightful prism through which we see a delicate dance of fireflies and countless other wonders — poems, haiku and translations to illuminate the heart and the world."

~ GABRIEL ROSENSTOCK
author of *Haiku Enlightenment*
and *Bliain an Bhandé / Year of the Goddess*

"Ivan M. Granger has thrown open the doors of his body, heart and mind to the Infinite's expressions of Itself in this world... These poems touch all the heart-strings. I laughed, I shed tears, I fell into contemplative states, I felt awe and wonder, love and longing as I read his offerings... You'll want to return to this wellspring to quench your thirst over and over again."

~ LAWRENCE EDWARDS, Ph.D.
author of *The Soul's Journey: Guidance From the Divine Within*
and *Kali's Bazaar*

REAL THIRST
POETRY OF THE SPIRITUAL JOURNEY

Poems & Translations by
Ivan M. Granger

POETRY CHAIKHANA

www.poetry-chaikhana.com

ISBN: 0985467940
ISBN-13: 978-0-9854679-4-4

Acknowledgements

This book was made possible with the encouragement and help of the Poetry Chaikhana online community – poetry lovers, cultural explorers, and spiritual seekers from every corner of the world. Thank you!

Special thanks to Aparna Sharma. Writers don't like to admit how much they benefit from the advice of a good editor. This is me admitting.

And my deepest thanks to my wife, Michele – wise woman, continuous source of inspiration.

"in love with the new sun" was first published in *Poems of Awakening: An International Anthology of Spiritual Poetry*, edited by Betsy Small.

"The Warbler Knows" has been published in Irish translation by Gabriel Rosenstock in his collection *Guthanna Beannaithe an Domhain: Imleabhar 2*

Ivan M. Granger's translation of "The Sum of Perfection" by John of the Cross was previously published in *For Lovers of God Everywhere: Poems of the Christian Mystics*, edited by Roger Housden.

The translation of Symeon the New Theologian's "The fire rises in me" was first published in *Nourishing the Teacher: Inquiries, Contemplations and Insights on the Path of Yoga*, by Danny Arguetty.

Several poems have been featured on the following websites: *Tiferet Journal, Poet Seers, Nonduality Highlights* and the *Poetry Chaikhana*.

CONTENTS

Foreword by Lawrence Edwards   i
Introduction by Dorothy Walters   ii

Surprised by the Sun   1
   First dawn / 2
   Parched / 3
   Every Shaped Thing / 4
   Medusa / 5
   carried by the wind / 7
   Autumn's first snow / 7
   Snow all day / 8
   beneath the spring moon / 10
   rainy day / 10
   listening / 10
   The Warbler Knows / 12
   Twelve Ways to Lose Your Head on Maui / 14
   Holy Ground / 17
   Thief of Hearts / 18
   No stars / 20
   Goodnight Moon / 21
   Prometheus / 22
   All You Gurus / 23
   Trinket / 26
   Naked / 27
   There Is No Letting Go / 28
   How Can I Explain? / 29
   Day and Night / 30
   Bent / 31
   Mountain Peaks / 32
   games in a green field / 32
   white world / 33
   Nameless / 34
   Too many nights / 35
   in love with the new sun / 36
   On the way / 37

Adi Atman 38

Translations 50

  Symeon the New Theologian / 51
    How is it I can love you / 53
    The fire rises in me / 54
    The Light of Your Way / 55
  Hakim Sanai / 57
    There is no place for place / 59
  Francis of Assisi / 60
    Prayer Before the Crucifix / 62
  John of the Cross / 63
    The Sum of Perfection / 65
    Dark Night / 66
  Tukaram / 68
    All men to me are god-like Gods / 69
  Sarmad / 70
    Every man who knows his secret / 72
  Bulleh Shah / 73
    One Thread Only / 74
  Sachal Sarmast / 75
    Friend, this is the only way / 76
  Vladimir Solovyov / 76
    Three Meetings (excerpt) / 79
  Tulsi Sahib / 80
    Within This Body / 81
  Antonio Machado / 82
    Songs / 83

Notes 88

FOREWORD BY LAWRENCE EDWARDS

Ivan M. Granger has thrown open the doors of his body, heart and mind to the Infinite's expressions of Itself in this world. *Real Thirst*, the book and the title poem, are shimmering examples of his loving dedication. His life and offerings of selfless service are too, and truly not to be separated from this work. They prepare the opening for the winds and light of the Infinite to move through and create forms Ivan is compelled to give substance to. Because of that he can write:

> The parched know –
>
> real thirst
> draws rainwater
> from an empty sky.

We are the beneficiaries of his efforts to part Medusa's locks, to look into the unwavering stare of the Dark Goddess, whose gifts go to those who are ready to go beyond the snakes of the mind, and die to the ordinary world in order to journey beyond. The gifts of this hero's return are the poems of *Real Thirst*.

These poems touch all the heart-strings. I laughed, I shed tears, I fell into contemplative states, I felt awe and wonder, love and longing as I read his offerings. All I can say to you is take possession of Ivan's gifts, imbibe what he has labored to give you, that you may know these truths directly for yourself. You'll want to return to this wellspring to quench your thirst over and over again.

> Lawrence Edwards, Ph.D.
> Founder & Director of *The Anam Cara Foundation*
> Founder & Director of *Optimal Mind®*

INTRODUCTION BY DOROTHY WALTERS

Some years ago, shortly after I had published my first volume of verse, I received a letter from a correspondent named Ivan Granger. Somehow he had discovered my book and was requesting permission to publish a few of my poems on his new website called "Poetry Chaikhana." I was honored by his request and of course consented immediately, but I was also a bit puzzled by the title of his venture. Ultimately I learned that a "chaikhana" is a teahouse ("chai" plus "stopping place"). Such places of refreshment were common on the old trade routes of the Middle East, locations where travelers could be refreshed not only by food and tea but also by entertainment, including the exchange of poetry.

Ivan's Poetry Chaikhana has now existed for many years. Within this teahouse, he publishes spiritual poetry from many traditions and nationalities, many from earlier eras. In addition he presents music as well as an original "thought for the day." These inspirational offerings are available free of charge to anyone subscribing to his e-mail list. As a result, his readership has grown to many thousands of readers over the globe. This contribution to the spiritual growth of so many is truly impressive.

In the course of this work, Ivan Granger has mined the spiritual literature of countless poets of myriad eras and locales. He has unearthed and brought to light a host of early voices virtually unknown in the modern Western world.

Now and again, Ivan has given us glimpses of his own poetic gifts, for he is very much a poet in his own right as well as a connoisseur of the work of others. But not until this current collection of his own work appeared did the evidence emerge so clearly of just how significant these were, nor did we realize that we had among us a poet of such spiritual depth and power.

Ivan presents in the present volume a variety of forms and approaches, but the unifying essence of the whole is his own sensibility and perception, always imbued with the respect and even reverence that such poems of the sacred require. At times he relies on familiar traditional forms (such as the various haiku poems in which succinctness leads to unexpected revelation). Again, he creates forms appropriate to subject, and offers more extended poetic investigations of his themes. His approach is "spiritual" in the finest sense of the term, one not handicapped by various "new age" appropriations of the term. His poetry is crafted, polished, and above all authentic.

Such voices working out of the spiritual tradition are a rarity in our time. Consider, for example:

Holy Ground

Let the vision
of the vastness
you are
leave you
in glorious
ruins.

Pilgrims will come
to imagine
the grand temple
that once stood,
not realizing
    the wreck
    made this empty plain
    holy ground.

Only one who has made the journey, stood in the holy fire, and discovered the immensity of the Mystery itself could write such lines. Ivan realizes that the sacred journey is not a joy ride into the proffered pleasure of instant liberation, but rather a constant humbling and even obliteration of self before the Holy Spirit, which he does not name but nonetheless is present in its great "vastness."

Again, there is the brief but moving poem titled "Thief of Hearts," which captures the sense that the "Holy Thief" removes all sense of prior self and ordinary considerations, leaving behind only a few telltale reminders of the "robbery" which has occurred. In this regard, the poem reminds us that this feeling of "sacred loss" characterizes the journey of mystics of all times.

Thief of hearts,
you have ransacked
this beggar's hut,
left me
nothing.

All I see
now

is the print
of your pilfering hand
everywhere.

But the serious poems are often balanced by others of a more playful
tone, as in the lighter sequence named "All You Gurus," which contains
the delightful verse:

All you gurus –

Beware the diligent disciple.
Ceaselessly meditating,
he has already tried
your back door.

And then there is the humorous poem "Bent," long one of my favorites,
recalling as it does the constant admonition to students that they keep
the spine straight when they perform yoga or other physical/spiritual
practices:

Yes, seekers, do
sit up,
stand tall.

But hear
my bent secret:

All saints slouch.

God's lovers lean
into the divine embrace
and there
let the years pass...

In the eloquent sequence "Adi Atman" Ivan returns to a more serious
approach. As he himself explains in his notes, "Adi Atman isn't really a
proper name; it can be translated as 'the primal Self,' the heart of all
being. So this poem is the voice of the small self complaining to the
Eternal..."

Adi Atman,

your brush is dipped
in black

black hairs drinking black
black hairs rolled
against gray stone
black hairs rolled
to a fine black tip

white
beneath your black
brush –
I wait

I wait
your first mark
– quick and rough

will I know myself
after?

In addition to his own poems, Ivan offers a unique selection of the many translations he has done from an array of devotional writers representing various traditions and locales. Included among these are renderings of the poems of Symeon the New Theologian (Turkey), Hakim Sanai (Afghanistan), Francis of Assisi (Italy), John of the Cross (Spain), Tukaram (India), Sarmad (Iran), Sachal Sarmast (Pakistan/India), Bulleh Shah (Pakistan/India), Vladimir Solovyov (Russia), Tulsi Sahib (India), and Antonio Machado (Spain).

Each of these is a gem in its own right, and the total collection reminds us that love of the divine has no boundaries or time barriers but exists from the earliest eras as well as characterizing the modern scene. Some of Ivan's renditions will be from familiar authors, others will be new discoveries for some readers.

This book offers abundant inspiration and fresh insight into the world of the authentic pilgrim, a figure becoming more and more rare in modern times. It is a unique presentation from one who is both scholar and mystic, original poet and collector of others' works. *Real Thirst* should be in the library of any serious seeker on the path. It should be read aloud from pulpits and savored in the midnight devotions of the solitary seeker. It reminds us of who we are, our origins and destinies as spirits inhabiting for a time material bodies on the planet called Earth.

Dorothy Walters, Ph.D.
Colorado, 2012

SURPRISED BY THE SUN

First dawn. Even the
birds in the tallest pines are
surprised by the sun.

Parched

The parched know —

real thirst
draws rainwater
from an empty sky.

Every Shaped Thing

Sighing,
every shaped thing
turns
heavenward.

Your altar
cannot seat
the thousand thousand
idols.

Holding them,
what do you have?

Each gilded god
says:

"I am
impoverished
by the sun.

I can only
point
up."

Medusa

Medusa says –

I was wisdom
once,
black as night.

Now they call me:
      monster,
      gorgon,
      hideous-faced.

So I hide
behind this hissing curtain
of hair.

Lost
little ones,
breathe easy;
you are free
to not see.

But
what is a lonely
old lady to do?

I still wait
for some daughter,
      some son,
so wounded by the world,
to seize these snakes
and part my locks wide.

I still wait
for some bold, tired
      wild child of mine,

determined to die
seeing what's reflected
in my unblinking eye.

carried by the wind
a lone maple leaf dances
to an unknown home

Autumn's first snow.
Crimson leaves lined in white,
too much color to cover.

Snow all day.
Field, lake, and sky
withdraw into white.

Stumble
and so see the sky.

beneath the Spring Moon
the darting rook discovers
how to disappear

Rainy day.
Ghosts, forgotten friends
tapping at my window

listening to the rain
even horses settle
into themselves

When we are wise, we shape
neither sight nor self;
we lose ourselves, instead.

Somehow the battered heart
blossoms with such beauty,
no hint of past hurts.

The Warbler Knows

The warbler knows
only dawn's shaft
of light
on her breast.

Forgetting false future
suns, she sings

in no voice
but her own.

We dance along the seam of connection.

Twelve Ways to Lose Your Head on Maui

I.
Piercing the clouds, fingers
of sunlight caress the valley floor.
The Iao Needle stands, its immense
      quiet crushing.

        II.
        Staring blindly out the window,
        no work getting done –
        a stolen moment when silence
            has stolen me.

III.
Reading, I shiver in the Upcountry chill.
Already old in the new year, the island
and I shiver
      and grow still.

        IV.
        Baldwin Avenue meandering to Paia
        beneath an empty sky,
        cane fields
            surge in the sun.

V.
At the altar: Breath
aglow in my throat.
Golden treacle pools
      upon my heart.

        VI.
        The path to Twin Falls, dusty
        between my toes. Wild ginger points
        to the upper pool. Fallen guavas
            float downstream.

VII.
Hana Highway, pausing
at each bridge to let traffic pass.
Around the bend –
      endless ocean.

           VIII.
           Fasting on Saturday –
           empty stomach, empty head.
           Time spreads
                 into stillness.

IX.
Cinnamon-red and blue, a pheasant stares
through the window. My wife
calls me, whisper. I see them
      see each other.

           X.
           In the cave among the eucalyptus
           up Alae Road – a fine seat
           for a city boy
               playing sadhu.

XI.
In bursts of wingbeats
a cardinal darts by. The red
bird finds himself lost
      among the red proteas.

           XII.
           The sun setting beyond
           Ma'alaea Harbor. The golden
           ocean,
           I see, drinks the tired eye in.
             I am gone.

Love the mountain
more than the map.

Holy Ground

Let the vision
of the vastness
you are
leave you
in glorious
ruins.

Pilgrims will come
to imagine
the grand temple
that once stood,
not realizing

        the wreck
        made this empty plain
        holy ground.

Thief of hearts,
you have ransacked
this beggar's hut,
left me
nothing.

All I see
now
is the print
of your pilfering hand
everywhere.

Seeking sunlight
the sapling

reaches out for that golden touch.

In time the tree
becomes the pathway of its own
seeking.

No stars, just the dance
of fireflies to lead me
through this glowing world

Goodnight Moon

Beloved, tell me –

Why do you come
only when I
orphan my ambitions?

Why do you show
only when all hope
has fled?

Why, Honeyed Moon,
will you meet me
only on my funeral bed?

And, tell me –

Why won't the dead
stay dead?

Prometheus

The arsonist's eye
sees
in every stick
only sleeping flame.

It sees
each twig
fulfill itself
in fire.

This world
trembles
at heaven's
all-consuming
stare.

Yet Prometheus suffers
bound
to his black rock.

With his lightning blind wit
he gave fire to the world –

rather than give the world to it.

All You Gurus

All you gurus –

Beware the poet.
He sings
your praises,
spreading delightful
lies
and not caring.

All you gurus –

Beware the scholar.
With devotion
he records
your entire history
when you have
none.

All you gurus –

Beware the priest.
He builds
spired temples
on every green hilltop
only to house
himself.

All you gurus –

Beware the girl.
She casts her look,
hoping, terrified,
you will take the hook.

All you gurus –

Beware your wife.
She serves all
with eyes of compassion
fixed
on the softest seat.

All you gurus –

Beware the diligent
disciple.
Ceaselessly meditating,
he has already tried
your back door.

Gurus, beware
these children
in your care.
They teach you
how much of you
is still there.

The encounters of this moment
fill the world.

Trinket

Mother,
you are too practical,

trying to put
this odd lump
to good use.

Melt me down.

Make of me
some golden trinket,
some frivolous, bejeweled thing
to please
your eye.

Hang me
from your ear;
let me rest
against the warm pulse
of your neck.

Go ahead, Mother,
it is just you and I
before the mirror.
I won't tell
if you want to spin
and laugh
like a girl
to see
this bit of glitter
set off
your smile.

Naked

We are mapped
in stitched flesh,
ragged sighs.

The naked
know the way.

Learning love's fierce art,
the naked walk
the blood trail

in silence

to the heart.

There Is No Letting Go

There is no
letting go.

Even your absence
touches me.

The new moon
is not gone;

she hides
her face
      in the night.

How Can I Explain?

Beloved, they want to know:
Did I reach up to You,
or did You reach out to me?

And they want to know:
What is real
touch?

How can I explain

— we pour
into each other.

Day and Night

You are:

shining, changeless
bliss,

tasting
neither death
nor birth.

The sun
does not rise
eager, bright-eyed;

there is
no tired, crimson pyre
heralding the stars.

Day and night –

they exist
only for the spinning
world.

The most mundane things open themselves
into infinities.

Bent

Yes, seekers, do
sit up,
stand tall.

But hear
my bent secret:

    All saints slouch.

God's lovers lean
into the divine embrace
and there
let the years pass.

    Struggling for straightness,
    your strivings shaken,

    learn what true knowers know:

Effort clears the way,
but the steps
are already taken.

Mountain Peaks

Why is it among the most
glacial mountain peaks
I find
the greatest warmth?

Games in a green field,
children at noon. The only
quiet - my shadow.

white world

i can still see them
when the mist
draws about

the eucalyptus
the wattle in flower

but they are not quite
there

fog sails
across the grass

but the white world
is still

Nameless

There is one
too big
for words,

his name
spoken
only in

silence.
Naked,

he taunts
the universe
to clothe him.

Too many nights
and no moon.

Have you stopped
heaven and earth
to hide your face?

If you will not
drench me
in your light

then swallow me
in this blind
hunger!

See everything
with a fierce eye
and a gentle heart.

in love with the new sun
the cherry blossom forgets
the night's frost

On the way
home
I stop

ADI ATMAN

Adi Atman,

your brush is dipped
in black
      black hairs drinking black
      black hairs rolled
against gray stone
      black hairs rolled
to a fine black tip

white
beneath your black
brush –
I wait

I wait
your first mark
– quick and rough

will I know myself
after?

Adi Atman,

was it you
with measuring
brown eyes?

you who could walk
upon the shoulders
of stone giants?

and disappear
so completely?

it must have been raining
the day you left,
heavy drops
scoring the tasteless air
in their drive to the earth

and losing you
I knew
for the first time
what it was
to search

a hard blessing

Adi Atman,

2 AM
the witch's midnight

2 AM
and even crows sleep
in the black tree tops
even the crows sleep
from their gabbling efforts
leading the dead to the dead

2 AM
and even cats sleep
wound warm
atop blackened television sets

2 AM
and the empty streets hum
beneath the full moon

Witch!
Enchanter!
it is 2 AM
and I cannot sleep
your spell keeps me
awake

Adi Atman,

stop pushing

every time
you set your foot
upon the plain

I have lost
a home

Adi Atman,

who did I think you were
when I spilled my blood
on the red Sonoran rocks?

a black eagle
thirsting for blood
ready to pluck
my beating heart
from its cage?

I was crazy from thirst!
I pierced
myself for you
caught in ocotillo
slung from saguaro.

why didn't you
stop me?

Adi Atman,

I sought your vixen eyes
in the glance of my first lover

I sought your breath
upon her lips
and your secret
in the way she was
blanketed by the night

she betrayed me –
by remaining herself.

You betrayed me –
by remaining hidden
in plain sight

watching
our attempts
at coming together
coming apart

when a single word
from you
would have resolved
the whole matter

Adi Atman,

the game is up
the moon is climbing
the night sky

Adi Atman,

I was lost
among the bamboo
and the clouds
with the brooksong
in my ear

why did you show me
the way
back?

Adi Atman,

I am a fool

I place a picture
before me
and say
         – you you

hosanna hari hari bol!

daybreak and I whisper
to the sun
         – you

full moon night
and I cry out
         – you

summer downpour
the thunder crash
shouts for me
         – YOU

drowning
drunk from too much
seawater
I sputter
         – you you you

shambo shankara!

I am a grasping fool
I say – you –

and you are gone

when I remember to shut up
then you are here

and I am gone

Adi Atman,

the full moon has lit up
the countryside
showing me
every slope and shallow

yet I cannot see
my hand
in front of my face

TRANSLATIONS

SYMEON THE NEW THEOLOGIAN

949 – 1032
BYZANTINE EMPIRE (TURKEY)

Symeon was born into an aristocratic family in Asia Minor (Turkey) and was given the name George. At this time, the region was still part of the Christian Byzantine Empire. From boyhood George was groomed for a life in politics. As he entered adolescence, he was sent to the capital Constantinople (Istanbul) to live with his uncle who guided him in his early education.

When he.was 14 years old, George met a monk named Symeon the Pious. The monk became the boy's spiritual director. At the age of 20, George was overcome by an ecstatic state in which he experienced God as a living presence of radiant light.

Despite this radically transformative experience, he spent several more years attempting to fulfill his family's expectations, finally becoming an imperial senator. His continuing mystical experiences were not compatible with such a public life and, at the age of 27, he renounced his previous life and became a monk to continue under the direct guidance his spiritual director, even taking the same monastic name – Symeon.

In addition to taking monastic vows, he was later ordained a priest and eventually became the abbot of his monastery. As abbot, he revived the monastery's life of prayer and introspection.

The mystical spiritual practices Symeon advocated led to further conflicts with authorities and he was exiled in 1009 to a small hermitage on the far side of the Bosphorus, the strait of water near Constantinople that separates the Near East from Europe.

Disciples began to gather around Symeon and soon the small hermitage grew into a full monastery. It was there that Symeon wrote his most personal work, Hymns of Divine Love, *a collection of poems describing his mystical experiences.*

How is it I can love You
        within me,
        yet see You from afar?

How is it I embrace You
        within myself,
        yet see you spread across the heavens?

You know. You alone.
        You, who made this mystery,
        You who shine
like the sun in my breast,
        You who shine
        in my material heart,
                immaterially.

The fire rises in me,
        and lights up my heart.
Like the sun!
Like the golden disk!
Opening, expanding, radiant –
        Yes!
        – a flame!

I say again:
        I don't know
        what to say!

I'd fall silent
– If only I could –
but this marvel
        makes my heart leap,
it leaves me open mouthed
        like a fool,

urging me
        to summon words
        from my silence.

The Light of Your Way

You have flooded my heart
      with the light of your way,

and you have raised up in me
      the Tree of Life.

You have shown me a new heaven
      upon the earth.
You have shown me a secret Garden,
      unseen within the seen.

Now am I joined soul and spirit
      present in your Presence –

your Presence that has waited long in me,
your Presence, the true Tree of Life,
      planted in whatever this earth is,
      planted in whatever it is that men are,
         planted, and rooted in the heart,

your Presence all at once revealing your Paradise
alive with every good green thing:
      grasses and trees and the fruiting bounty,
      a world of flowers!
         sweet-scented lilies!

Each little flower speaks a truth:
      humility and joy,
      peace, oh peace!
      kindness, compassion,
         the turning of the soul,

and the flood of tears
and the strange ecstasy
     of those bathed in your light.

HAKIM SANAI

1044? – 1150?
AFGHANISTAN

Hakim Sanai was born in the province of Ghazna in southern Afghanistan in the middle of the 11th century and probably died around 1150.

Sanai was originally a court poet who was engaged in writing praises for the Sultan of Ghazna. A story is told of how the Sultan decided to lead a military attack against neighboring India, and Sanai, as a court poet, was summoned to join the expedition to record the Sultan's exploits. As Sanai was making his way to the court, he passed an enclosed garden frequented by a notorious drunk named Lai Khur.

Passing by, Sanai heard Lai Khur loudly proclaim a toast to the blindness of the Sultan for greedily choosing to attack India, when there was so much beauty in Ghazna. Sanai was shocked and stopped. Lai Khur then proposed a toast to the blindness of the famous young poet Sanai who, with his gifts of insight and expression, couldn't see the pointlessness of his existence as a poet praising such a foolish Sultan.

These words hit Sanai like an earthquake. He knew they were true. He abandoned his life as a pampered court poet, even declining marriage to the Sultan's own sister, and dedicated himself to the inner path of Sufism.

Soon after, Sanai went on pilgrimage to Mecca. When he returned, he composed his poetic masterpiece, The Walled Garden of Truth.

There is a double meaning in the title for, in Persian, the word for a garden also means paradise, yet it was from within a garden that Lai Khur uttered the harsh truths that set Hakim Sanai on the path of wisdom.

There is no place for place!
How can a place
house the maker of all space,
or the vast sky enclose
        the maker of heaven?

He told me:
"I am a homeless treasure.
The world was made
to give you a place to stand
        and see me."

Tell me, if the one you seek
is placeless,
why put your shoes on?
The real road
is found by polishing, polishing
        the mirror of your heart.

FRANCIS OF ASSISI

1181 – 1226
ITALY

Francis was born in 1181 or 1182 to a prosperous merchant family in Assisi, Italy. As he grew up, his natural charm attracted people to him. He became a natural leader to a group of raucous young men. He led an easy, high spirited life, typical of a wealthy heir.

Francis's father dreamed of more than wealth for his son; he wanted his son to be elevated to nobility. Showing valor in war was the most likely way to accomplish this. The opportunity for this presented itself when a call went out for soldiers to go on crusade. Francis, his mind filled with romantic stories and aspirations for glory, bought a fine horse, had an elaborate suit of armor made, and left for war.

But he hadn't been more than a day's ride away when he had a dream in which God asked him to return home. He did so at once. This shocking action was interpreted by the townspeople as cowardice. His father was outraged at the family's humiliation and the money wasted.

Francis began to turn inward, devoting increasing time to prayer and wandering through the countryside.

While praying at the dilapidated church of San Damiano, Francis heard Christ say to him, "Go, Francis, and repair my house." Francis took this literally, and immediately began to rebuild the small church's crumbling walls. Only later would he interpret this command as a call to rebuild the spiritual foundations of the Church – Christian spirituality.

Francis bundled up loads of cloth from his father's shop and sold them to pay for these new endeavors, without permission. His father was enraged and called him before the presence of the local bishop, demanding that his son return the stolen money and renounce his rights as family heir.

Francis surprised everyone by stripping naked in the town square, declaring he would live by God's grace alone from that point onward. This, from the wild young man who had led gangs of carousing boys through the streets!

Francis's charisma never left him, even as he adopted a life of prayer, radical poverty, and service to the sick and the poor. Followers quickly gathered about him. Many were his former friends, the sons of wealthy and noble families.

Soon, the number of his followers had grown to such an extent that things became political with the Church. His mystical nature, his popularity with the poor, and his insistence on Christ's poverty was not liked by many within the Church, for it seemed to ally him with other mendicant esoteric groups that had been declared heretical.

In order to keep his followers from suffering a similar fate of suppression, he had to make it clear that he was well within the Church orthodoxy. He navigated a careful path, maintaining his essential message while avoiding overt criticism of Church excesses. He also had to seek formal recognition of his order by the Pope, which he finally received.

Francis's health was never good, and it worsened as he returned to a simple life of prayer and retreat. It was also during this time that he received the stigmata, Christ's wounds, while praying among a group of caves in the countryside.

Francis died in 1226 at the age of 45 and was immediately acclaimed to be a saint by the general population.

Prayer Before the Crucifix

Most high,
glorious God,
let your light fill the shadows of my heart
and grant me, Lord,
true faith,
certain hope,
perfect love,
awareness and knowing,
that I may fulfill Your holy will.

JOHN OF THE CROSS

1542 — 1591
SPAIN

*John of the Cross was born Juan de Ypes in a village near Avila,
Spain. His father died when he was young, and he was raised in
poverty with his two brothers by his widowed mother. His
intellectual gifts, however, were recognized by a patron who
provided for his early education at a Jesuit school.*

*In his early 20s, John entered the Carmelite order and moved to
Salamanca to further his studies. Among his other teachers was the
well-known mystic and poet Fray Luis de Leon.*

*Still in his 20s, the young John of the Cross first met the woman
who would become his mentor, Teresa of Avila, who was in her 50s
at the time. Teresa of Avila was a mystic, a writer, a social activist,
and the founder of several monasteries. She had begun a reform
movement within the Carmelite Order, advocating a return to
simplicity and the essential spirituality that should be at the heart of
a monastic order. John of the Cross joined her movement of
Discalced Carmelites and quickly became a leading figure himself.*

*Members of the unreformed Carmelites felt threatened by the
critique from this new movement, and they turned to force,
imprisoning and even torturing John of the Cross. He was held in a
tiny cell in Toledo for nine months, until he escaped.*

*As terrible as this experience must have been, it was during his time
of imprisonment that John's spirituality and poetry blossomed. The
experience of losing everything, of being supremely vulnerable,
seems to have brought John of the Cross to a profound state of*

openness and spiritual insight. One of his guards smuggled in scraps of paper, and John began to write poetry.

Free from prison, John continued his work with Teresa of Avila, founding new monasteries and advocating for their spiritual reforms. He spent the rest of his life as a spiritual director among the Discalced Carmelites.

His two best known works, the Spiritual Canticle and Dark Night of the Soul, are considered masterpieces of Spanish poetry and esoteric Christianity. Besides these, he wrote many other short poems, along with extensive commentaries on the meaning of his poetry as they relate to the soul's journey to God.

La Suma de la Perfección   **The Sum of Perfection**

Olvido de lo criado,   Creation forgotten,
memoria del Criador,   Creator only known,
atención a lo interior   Attention turned inward
y estarse amando al Amado.   In love with the Beloved alone.

Dark Night

(Songs of the soul delighted at having reached the high state of perfection, the union with God, by way of spiritual negation.)

On a darkened night,
Anxious, by love inflamed,
– O happy chance! –
Unnoticed, I took flight,
My house at last at peace and quiet.

Safe, disguised by the night,
By the secret ladder I took flight,
– O happy chance! –
Cloaked by darkness, I scaled the height,
My house at last at peace and quiet.

On that blessed night,
In secret, and seen by none,
None in sight,
I saw with no other guide or light,
But the one burning in my heart bright.

This guide, this light,
Brighter than the midday sun,
Led me to the waiting One
I knew so well – my delight!
To a place with none in sight.

O night! O guide!
O night more loving than the dawn!
O night that joined
The lover with the Beloved;
Transformed, the lover into the Beloved drawn!

Upon my flowered breast,
For him alone kept fair,
There he slept,
There I caressed,
There the cedars gave us air.

I drank the turret's cool air,
Spreading playfully his hair.
And his hand, so serene,
Cut my throat. Drained
Of senses, I dropped unaware.

Lost to myself and yet remaining,
Inclined so only the Beloved I spy.
All has ceased, all rests,
Even my cares, even I;
Lost among the lilies, there I die.

TUKARAM

1608 – 1649
INDIA

Tukaram was born in Maharashtra, in the western region of India, to a lower caste Shudra family. Despite being of a lower caste, the family was wealthy by rural standards.

When Tukaram was 13 years old, his father fell ill and the boy had to take on the responsibility of supporting his family. Soon after, both parents died.

Hardship continued to follow Tukaram. His first wife died during a famine, and his second wife had no respect for his devotion to God.

Contrary to the traditional Hindu model of receiving spiritual initiation from a guru, Tukaram was initiated in a dream by Lord Hari (Krishna/Vishnu) Himself.

When Tukaram sensed his end approaching, he stepped into a river, as many other saints have done. It is said that his rug and other belongings returned to shore, but his body was never found. Devotees believe he was taken bodily to heaven.

During Tukaram's relatively short life, he was constantly singing devotional hymns called abhangs. *He composed over 5,000 of these sacred hymns.*

All men to me are god-like Gods!
      My eyes no longer see
      vice or fault.

Life on this suffering earth
      is now endless delight;
      the heart at rest and full,
                    overflowing.

In the mirror, the face and its reflection
      watch each other;
      different, but one.

And, when the stream pours into the ocean...
      no more stream!

SARMAD

? – 1659
PERSIA (IRAN) & INDIA

Sarmad (sometimes called Sarmad the Cheerful or Sarmad the Martyr), is a fascinating and complex character who seems to have bridged several cultures in Persia and India. Apparently, Sarmad originally lived in the Kashan region in Iran, lying between Tehran and Isfahan. He was from a minority community of the society. Some biographies claim Sarmad was originally from a Jewish merchant family, though others say he was Armenian. Because of his possible Jewish heritage and his later migration to Delhi, he has been called the Jewish Sufi Saint of India.

Sarmad had an excellent command of both Persian and Arabic, essential for his work as a merchant. Hearing that precious items and works of art were being purchased in India at high prices, Sarmad gathered together his wares and traveled to India where he intended to sell them.

Near the end of his journey, however, he met a beautiful Indian boy and was entranced. This ardent love ('ishq) created such a radical transformation in his awareness that Sarmad immediately dropped all desire for wealth and worldly comfort. In his ecstatic state, Sarmad abandoned his considerable wealth and, losing all concern for social convention, he even began to wander about without clothes, becoming a naked faqir.

Some biographers assert that Sarmad formally converted to Islam, while others claim he had a universalist notion of God and religion, seeing no conflict between his Judaism and the Sufi path he adopted. In his own poetry, Sarmad asserts that he is neither Jew, nor Muslim, nor Hindu.

Sarmad continued to journey through India, but now as a naked dervish rather than as a merchant. He ended up in Delhi where he found the favor of a prince in the region and gained a certain amount of influence at court. That prince, however, was soon overthrown by Aurengzeb. The new king and orthodox religious authorities were offended by Sarmad's open criticism of their social hypocrisy and mindless religious formalism.

Aurengzeb, in fear of the people's love for Sarmad, staged a show trial. Sarmad was initially accused of breaking an injunction against public nudity, but that was later dropped in favor of the charges of atheism and unorthodox religious practices, for which he was convicted. The army was called in to occupy Delhi and prevent a popular uprising, and the naked saint was publicly beheaded. The story is told that, after the beheading, Sarmad's body picked up its own head which recited the Muslim affirmation of faith: "There is no god but God, and Muhammad is his Prophet." He then proclaimed to the crowd, "Ana al-Haq" ("I am Reality, I am one with God"), a statement famously made by another beloved Sufi martyr, Mansur al-Hallaj. Sarmad thus affirms the continuing stream of truth despite violent repression.

Sarmad's tomb in Delhi is today visited by pilgrims of all faiths: Muslim, Jewish, Hindu, Sikh, and others.

Every man who knows his secret
becomes a secret,
      hidden from the skies.

The sage says Ahmad rose to the heavens;
Sarmad says the heavens
      rose in him!

BULLEH SHAH

1680 – 1758
PUNJAB (PAKISTAN / INDIA)

Mir Bulleh Shah Qadiri Shatari, usually known as Bulleh Shah, lived in what is today Pakistan. His family was very religious and had a long tradition of association with Sufis. Bulleh Shah's father was especially known for his learning and devotion to God, raising both Bulleh Shah and his sister in a life of prayer and meditation.

Bulleh Shah himself became a respected scholar, but he longed for true inner realization. Against the objections of his peers, he became a disciple of a famous master of the Qadiri Sufi lineage, who ultimately guided his student to deep mystical awakening.

The nature of Bulleh Shah's realization led to such profound egolessness and non-concern for social convention that it has been the source of many popular comical stories – calling to mind the antics of other famous divine fools, like St. Francis and Sri Ramakrishna. For example, one day Bulleh Shah watched a young woman eagerly awaiting the return of her husband. Bulleh Shah deeply identified with the devoted way she prepared herself for her beloved. Inspired, Bulleh Shah dressed himself as a woman and braided his own hair, as he had seen the young woman do, before he hurried to see his spiritual teacher.

Bulleh Shah is considered to be one of the greatest mystic poets of the Punjab region.

One Thread Only

One thread, one thread only!
Warp and woof, quill and shuttle,
countless cloths and colors,

> a thousand hanks and skeins –
> with ten thousand names
> ten thousand places.

But there is one thread only.

SACHAL SARMAST

1739 – 1829
PAKISTAN / INDIA

Sachal Sarmast urged people to seek the truth directly, rather than through mere conformity to tradition. He taught a Sufi vision of unity which has been compared to the great nondualist teachings of Advaita Vedanta within Hinduism and Zen/Ch'an within Buddhism.

He was born Abdul Wahab in the Sindh region of what is today Pakistan. His father died when he was a young child, and the boy was raised by his uncle, who also became his spiritual master.

His soul was deeply moved by music. Listening to music sent him into a state of rapture with tears pouring down his face.

He married, but his young wife died two years later. He never remarried.

Abdul Wahab took the name Sachal (Truth). Later people added Sarmast (Leader of the Ecstatics) to his name in appreciation of his spiritual poetry. He is sometimes called Sachoo, The Truthful.

Sachal Sarmast lived a humble, ascetic life, preferring solitude, simple meals of dhal and yogurt. It is said that he never left the village of his birth, yet he composed sacred poetry in seven different languages, poetry that is loved and sung to this day.

Friend, this is the only way
to learn the secret way:

Ignore the paths of others,
even the saints' steep trails.

Don't follow.
Don't journey at all.

Rip the veil from your face.

VLADIMIR SOLOVYOV

1853 – 1900
RUSSIA

Vladimir Sergeyevich Solovyov (sometimes written in English as Soloviev) was a philosopher, poet, literary critic, and mystic with an intense connection to the divine feminine archetype of Sophia or Holy Wisdom. His writings had a strong influence on Russian Symbolist poetry and on Russian spirituality in general in the early 20th century.

Solovyov was born in Moscow in 1853. His father was a famous historian and a professor at Moscow University. At the age of nine, triggered by the early longings of love for a girl, Solovyov had the first in a series of three mystical encounters with Sophia.

By the time he was 13 years old, in spite of this early visionary experience, Solovyov had entered a period of spiritual crisis in which he renounced the Orthodox Church and began what he described as a troubled exploration of materialism and nihilism. He initially studied natural history and biology at university, but his grades began to slip. He switched to studies in history and philosophy.

Sometime in his early 20s, he "reconverted" to the Orthodox Church, and became a lay theological student and lecturer.

It was about this time, while in London studying at the British Museum, that Solovyov had his second encounter with Sophia, where he saw her face. Pleading with her to allow her full form to be seen, Solovyov received a response to meet her in Egypt. He went to Egypt where Sophia appeared to him in the desert at dawn. She revealed to him a vision of the Earth transfigured, a vision with all nature, all things, unified within her form as the Divine Feminine.

After his return to Russia, Solovyov briefly taught philosophy at Moscow University, but soon left because he disliked university politics. He then moved to St. Petersberg where he wrote and taught.

Solovyov taught an engaged Christianity of service and activism, in which the binding power of Sophia – the Mother/Wisdom/Love nature of God – could heal the world. For Solovyov, art could be a modern form of prophecy to bring greater awareness of this mystical unity to humanity.

Among his many works of poetry, his masterpiece is Tri Svidaniya *or "Three Meetings" describing his three mystical encounters with Sophia. In his writings, Solvyov describes his encounters with Sophia as being filled with radiant azure and violet light.*

Solovyov was friends with the great Russian novelist, Fyodor Dostoevsky.

Three Meetings (excerpt)

Agown in heavenly purple glow you stood,
Eyes full of azure fire,
Your vision was the first blaze
Of world-filling, life-giving day.

What is, what was, what shall forever be –
All, all was held here in one steady gaze...
The seas and rivers blue beneath me,
Distant woods, snow-capped peaks.

I saw all, and all was one –
A single image of womanly beauty...
Pregnant with vastnesses!
Before me, in me – only You.

Radiant One! You can't fool me:
I saw all of you there in the desert.
Those roses in my soul won't wilt,
Whichever way the day may turn.

Yet but an instant! And the vision veiled.
The sun climbed the sky's height.
Silence, desert silence. And so my soul prayed;
While within: an endless celebration of bells!

TULSI SAHIB

1763 – 1843
INDIA

Although Tulsi Sahib lived relatively recently, few details about his life can be stated with certainty. He may have been part of the royal family of Poona.

One biographical account suggests he was engaged to be married against his will. On the day before his wedding, he ran away and took up the life of a sadhu, *a spiritual mendicant wandering through forests, going from town to town, engaged in meditation. In the early 1800s, he settled in Hathras in Uttar Pradesh, where he spent the rest of his life.*

Tulsi Sahib practiced Surat Shabd Yoga, or the Yoga of Sound. He is particularly revered within the Sant Mat Sikh tradition.

Within This Body

Within this body
breathes the secret essence.
Within this body
beats the heart of the Vedas.

Within this body
shines the entire Universe,
      so the saints say.

Hermits, ascetics, celibates –
all are lost
seeking Him
      in endless guises.

Seers and sages perfectly parrot
the scriptures and holy books,
      blinded by knowledge.

      Their pilgrimage,
      and fasting,
      and striving
          but delude.
Despite their perfect practice,
they discover no destination.

Only the saints
who know the body's heart
have attained the Ultimate, O Tulsi.

Realize this, and you've found your freedom
      (while teachers trapped in tradition
      know only the mirage
          in the mirror).

ANTONIO MACHADO

1875 – 1930
SPAIN

*With most of Antonio Machado's poetry, the land itself is his
primary subject. For Machado, the countryside is alive, the central
presence that awakens a deeper, somewhat melancholy awareness
of all that is.*

*Antonio Machado's wife died when she was very young. It is through
his lifelong anguish over this loss that a kind of spiritual yearning
emerges. He begins to see his dead wife as his divine beloved, ever
present, ever calling to him, yet ever just out of reach. The goal of
union can only be found within. In this way, his terrible ache was
elevated to an experience of the sacred, similar perhaps to that
sought through the ideal of "courtly love" espoused by the
Troubadours several centuries earlier.*

*When his poetry speaks of this beloved woman, read into it the
divine, and see what meaning emerges.*

Songs

I

      Against the flowering mountain,
the wide sea surges.
The comb of my honeybees
has gathered grains of salt.

           II

              Against the black water.
         Scent of sea and jasmine.
         Malaga night.

III

      Spring has come.
No one knows what has happened.

           IV

              Spring has come.
         White hallelujahs
         from the brambles in flower!

V

      Full moon, full moon,
so pregnant, so round.
This serene March night,
honeycomb of light
carved by white bees!

           VI

              Castile night;
         the song is said,
         or, better, unsaid.
         When all sleep
         I'll go to the window.

VII
  Sing, sing in clear rhyme,
the almond's green arm
and the river's double willow.

  Sing of the mottled oak,
the branch the ax cut,
and the flower no one sees.

  Of the garden pear's
white flower, the peach tree's
rosy blossom.

  And this perfume
the wet wind plucked
from the blossoming beans.

        VIII
          The fountain and the four
        acacias aflower
        in the plaza.
        The sun burns no more.
        Twilight bliss!
        Sing, nightingale.
        This is the hour
        of my heart.

IX
  White lodge,
traveler's cell,
with my shadow!

X
  The Roman waterway,
– sings a voice from my homeland –
and the love we have for each other,
little one, what strength!

XI
  With words of love
a bit of exaggeration
just feels right.

XII
  In Santo Domingo,
the high mass.
Even though they call me
heretic and Mason,
praying with you,
what devotion!

XIII
  Celebrations in the green pasture
– fife and drum.
With his flower-draped crook
and golden sandals a shepherd came.

  Down from the mountain I came,
only to dance with her;
to the mountain I'll return.

  Among the bower
there is a nightingale;
it sings of night and of day,
it sings of the moon and the sun.

Husky from song:
to the garden goes the girl
and a rose she will cut.

Between the black oaks,
there is a fountain of stone,
and a clay pitcher
that is never full.

By the oak wood,
with the white moon,
she will return.

XIV

      With you in Valonsadero,
Feast of San Juan,
morning in the Argentine plain,
on the other side of the sea.
Keep faith in me,
that I will return.

      Tomorrow I'll be the wind upon the
plain
and my heart itself will go
to the banks of the High Douro.

XV

While you are dancing in a circle,
girls, sing:
The fields are already green,
April in his splendor has come.

At the riverbank,
near the black oaks,
his silver sandals
we've seen shine.
The fields are already green,
April in his splendor has come.

NOTES

"Every Shaped Thing"
One morning, in my Maui days, I stepped outside to greet the sun. A forest of scattered eucalyptus trees stood before me, the slope of Haleakala Volcano rising behind me. A timeless moment. I sat there gazing about in a sweetly meditative state of mind, and I saw everything reaching, turning, pointing heavenward. All of creation, every person, every thing, even every idea – "every shaped thing" – is a reflection of the radiance present everywhere. Whenever we desire a thing or person or experience, what we crave is not the thing itself, but that spark barely glimpsed within it. It is never the object we actually seek, it is that shine. Seen clearly, everything is a mirror held up to the face of the Divine. The only real value anything has is in how it points back to its glowing source.

"Medusa"
I was surprised by something I discovered a few years back: Medusa, the quintessential monster of Greek mythology, was originally a much loved goddess. Her name comes from the Greek word "metis" (related to the Sanskrit "medha") meaning "wisdom." Her worship is thought to have originated in Northern Africa and been imported into early Greek culture. She was black-skinned, wore wild, matted hair (with, of course, snakes), stood naked, wide-eyed, and embodied the mystery of woman, the wisdom of the night, the truths too profound or terrible to face in the daylight. Medusa is, in effect, a Mediterranean version of the Indian Goddess Kali. Medusa was eventually subsumed into the safer, patriarchal worship of Athena, who carries Medusa's head upon her shield. This discovery inspired me to look at the figure of Medusa more deeply. What is the wisdom that terrifies? Why the snakes? Why the petrifying open-eyed stare? And how does such a bringer of terrible wisdom feel about being rejected by her children as a "monster"?

"Twelve Ways to Lose Your Head on Maui"
In 2000, my wife and I moved to the island of Maui, having never even visited the islands before. My first impression didn't match my vision of a tropical paradise at all. We arrived just after the cane harvest, so we were greeted with large tracts of exposed red earth. Driving through the surfer town of Paia for the first time, with red dust swirling around wood slat storefronts, it felt like we had arrived in the Australian outback. But, over time, I really came to love the *aina*, the land of Hawaii. I wasn't a beach dweller; we lived high up

along the slopes of Haleakala Volcano, among the misty forests of eucalyptus. Every human structure was a bit run down, but there was something... normal about that. Even the trophy mansions hidden behind iron gates felt somehow temporary, just passing through on a slow current. As I began to give in to the rhythms of life on the island, a quiet and ease settled into my body in a way I'd never known before. We lived there for four years before returning to the mainland. But I still have visions of looking down the slope of Haleakala, all the way down to Ma'alaea Harbor, while the heavy golden sun sinks in glory beneath the horizon...

"Thief of Hearts"

Let's face it, from the ego's point-of-view, the relationship with the Divine is a problematic one. What the heart recognizes as liberation, the ego sees as theft. So what is the ego to do when that master thief breaks in and reveals everything to be the filmy stuff of dreams and light? A note about the poem's structure: The poem itself is a pair of thieving hands. It has two groups of five lines: two hands, five fingers each.

"Goodnight Moon"

"Why won't the dead / stay dead?" Several of my poems make rather unsettling references to death, but I'm not death obsessed – really. Death can be a spiritual device. The creeping awareness of mortality can heighten the senses, opening us for fully to the present moment. Sacred poetry often portrays death from an upside-down perspective in which death is sought with a perverse enthusiasm. It's easy to get the idea that these crazy poets all have a death wish. The death sought, however, is the death of the small self, the false self, the ego. Startlingly, that "death" – which is a real experience – awakens us to a previously unknown and immense sense of life. The little self is replaced by a vast, borderless, blissful sense of Self. But, something not often acknowledged – the awareness of this larger Self is not always stable. Like the moon, the light of this recognition can wax and then wane. The briefly illumined mystic can be left feeling bereft, calling out in the night to the Beloved. Light – such a shattering, giddy kiss! – and then the returning shadow of the ego-self we thought was banished... That's when the question arises, "Why won't the dead / stay dead?" There is, of course, an answer: One must acclimate to the expanded Self while mastering the art of stepping free from the ego. Now repeat.

"Mountain Peaks"
I have lived in the mountains or near the mountains much of my life. Their towering presence anchors me. Seeing mountains, I feel at home. True, living up in the mountains can be bleak when the winter snows blanket everything, but there is something deeply satisfying in a world brought to its pure essentials. In meditation, too, the mind is pared to its essentials, where thoughts cease, the awareness grows quiet. Then, like the mountaintop, the world comes into such peaceful clarity. The strange thing is that in that glacial state a bubbling warmth and vitality rises in us. Expecting such stillness to be frozen and lifeless, we discover instead life, warmth, bliss.

"white world"
The "mist" of the poem's "white world" is the radiant light that shines throughout existence. That light can be described as a mist because it permeates everything with its whiteness while it obscures the surfaces of things, swallowing all objects into itself. We "can still see them" – objects, the world – "but they are / not quite / there" – but they no longer seem tangible or real in any sustained sense. Within that all-embracing light, everything becomes ghost-like, mere outlines of seeming tangibility. And, although the "fog sails / across the grass," although that light is seen to be flowing outward through all things, we simultaneously see that this world built of light is at complete rest, "the white world / is still."

"in love with the new sun"
I first shared this poem on the Internet a few years ago, and the responses were immediate and surprisingly personal. One young woman in San Francisco contacted me for permission to tattoo the poem across her ribs! That's humbling to me as a poet. This poem is a love note to the joyful, easy unfolding after the long, chilly night of difficulties and spiritual effort.

"On the way home"
This haiku-like poem is inspired by the first line of a friend's poem. In fact, it *is* the first line of his poem. With a few well-placed line breaks, it becomes, I hope, a self-obliterating poem in its own right. On the journey, we discover we are already home. Wherever we are, we have already arrived. It is then that the sense of "I" stops.

Adi Atman isn't really a proper name; it can be translated as "the primal Self," the heart of all being. So this poem is the voice of the small self complaining to the Eternal, while slowly yielding and opening... finally melting into that wider sense of Being.

"stop pushing"
Every time the fundamental Self – Adi Atman – is recognized, every time it is glimpsed upon the "plain" of awareness, less room is left for the ego. The ego becomes uneasy, questioning its ultimate security, wondering if it even exists at all. "I have lost a home." The ego drives the early stages of spiritual exploration, wanting to acquire a thing called "spirituality." But at some point in the process, the ego's home is threatened by the presence of the Eternal, by the "foot" of Adi Atman. We instinctively shout back, "Stop pushing!" A dilemma every seeker must face: Where do we find the courage to proceed when the ego sees its territory diminishing? If we *are* the ego, going further is death and unthinkable. If we go forward anyway, then we must not be the ego... but then what are we? The courageous seeker somehow manages to whisper to that mysterious figure, "Keep pushing anyway."

"I am a fool"
On the one hand, to say "you" is to acknowledge God, the Divine Presence. On the other hand, "you" pushes God away, externalizes the Divine, creates alienation. Of course, we don't really alienate God; we alienate ourselves from God. Name It, try to grasp It... and It is gone. What we seek is the Wholeness, not an external person or thing that the mind can define and hold. The Living Whole can't be grasped or possessed in this way. The only way to claim It is to be claimed by It. The only way to gain It is to lose ourselves within It amidst deep, deep silence. "when I remember to shut up / then you are here / and I am gone"

"the full moon has lit up"
The illumination perceived in the ecstasy of deep meditation is often expressed in poetry as the full moon. It is the soft light that illumines the land below when all is at rest. A shining light is witnessed, a luminescence permeating the still field of the mind. Drenched in such light, we see everything with quiet clarity, everything except ourselves. Strangely, we no longer see a "self" at all.

The Spanish poems (by John of the Cross and Antonio Machado) and the Russian poem (by Vladimir Solovyov) are my direct translations from the original languages. The other "translations" should more properly be termed "English renderings" – my own English versions triangulated using as many translations as I could find, further shaped by my own intuition and poetic sensibilities.

"Prayer Before the Crucifix" – Francis of Assisi
Notice that this poem is itself constructed in the form of a crucifix. The top, the head of the cross acknowledges God above all else: "Most high, / glorious God." The arms of the cross, where the heart is centered, invites light into the heart: "let your light fill the shadows of my heart." The rising length of the cross lists the necessary spiritual qualities that must be built one upon the other to enlighten the heart: "true faith, / certain hope, / perfect love, / awareness and knowing." Finally, the base, the foundation upon which this entire spiritual structure stands is the Divine will and the individual soul's desire to embody it: "that I may fulfill Your holy will."

"Every man who knows his secret" – Sarmad
Islamic religious tradition tells of the *Mi'raj* when the Prophet Mohammed (Ahmad) ascends to heaven where he converses with God and the prophets. Sarmad, with the mystic's instinct, turns this inward, declaring that the *Mi'raj* was not an external journey, but a journey within, for "the heavens were inside Ahmad!" This declaration makes the journey to heaven available to us all: We can all discover the same heavenly expanse within ourselves.

"One Thread Only" – Bulleh Shah
Think about this image Bulleh Shah has given us: I imagine a great loom, with colored yarn feeding into it from all direction, the shuttle shooting back and forth, producing a highway of cloth in dazzling patterns and colors. We look at a multicolored cloth and see green in one part and red in another, and we see them as different. The mind names them "green" and "red," and separates them into different categories. We've mentally taken our shears and cut up the cloth – seeing two where there is, in fact, only one. It requires a delicate balance of perception to appreciate the endless variety of existence without losing sight of the whole. Most of us learn to pull it apart into separate swatches. It is only in the interrelated patterns spread wide across the whole cloth that we witness the grand beauty of the design.

"Songs" – *Antonio Machado*

The woman Machado refers to in this poem is probably his wife. She was raised in a traditional Catholic family, where only a churchgoer was considered a suitable match. When he was courting her, Machado started going to church regularly. He says ironically, "praying with you / what devotion!" You can just picture his eyes turned from the altar to catch a glimpse of her face. Sadly, she died as a young woman, soon after they were married. In Machado's poetry, she takes on a ghost-like quality, haunting his memories, calling to him. It's as if he feels a connection with her otherworldly presence through the very pain of separation. His longing is itself the connection

ABOUT THE AUTHOR

Ivan M. Granger is the founder and editor of the *Poetry Chaikhana*, an online resource of sacred poetry from around the world. He has lived in Oregon, California, and Hawaii. He now makes his home in Colorado with his wife and two dogs.

"Poetry has an immediate effect on the mind. The simple act of reading poetry alters thought patterns and the shuttle of the breath. Poetry induces trance. Its words are chant. Its rhythms drumbeats. Its images become the icons of the inner eye. Poetry is more than a description of the sacred experience; it carries the experience itself."

Made in the USA
Lexington, KY
15 July 2012